STUDY

OF THE INTEGRAL
USE OF THE
ZAMBEZI RIVER

ISBN: 9781695886056

STUDY

OF THE INTEGRAL

USE OS THE

ZAMBEZI RIVER

Juan Sanz Sanz

CLARIFICATION:

In September 1984, after years of thorough studies, calculations and checks, Juan Sanz Sanz (1943 - 2019), announced, by mail and in his personal capacity, to the highest levels of the moment in several countries and world decision centres, its written conclusions about the possible integral use of the Zambezi River; then it seemed the most suitable of the ways so that the evaluation and the possible start-up of the ideas it provided would not be delayed.

The baggage that gave him his wisdom, due to the depth of the immersion he did for decades in Geography and History, together with the careful observation of how much was happening in those years throughout the Planet, then gave the author the necessary momentum.

Unfortunately, the very cultured man has just passed away, a self-taught man who many would not hesitate to describe as a prototype of a person close to the Renaissance, given the large amount of knowledge that he sought to enlarge throughout his existence.

It is good to remember again that we are talking about 1984, so, as in the present 21st century, the word weighed heavily against him, always present in a hierarchical excess society: self-taught.

Without moving a comma from his legacy, the work is now published for the first time under the title: STUDY OF THE INTEGRAL USE OF THE ZAMBEZI RIVER.

BIOGRAPHY:

Self-taught, Juan Sanz Sanz (1943-2019), devoted himself, from early youth, to unravelling the problems posed by the readings of historical events narrated by the various authors who frequently diverged from each other.

Geography was one of his great hobbies and reason for fervent study, not existing on the planet place, no matter how remote it was, that had not been fully informed.

The attentive follow-up of the social and political reality in which its existence took place resulted in proposals for water use on three continents and each of the projects was sent in its day to the places that were most suitable for its achievement.

Languages - French, English, Italian, Portuguese and German, in addition to his own, Spanish - had no secrets for him and thus he could fully enjoy the Literature written in them, another hobby in which, as an enlightened man, he found his peers.

In early youth the Spanish guitar and later the piano, were musical instruments to which he dedicated a great effort similar to the passion that the music awoke in him and thus, in maturity, with authentic devotion and delicacy, he interpreted beautiful pieces of Bach , Chopin, Debussy and Beethoven who contributed a lot to make their days more human and the passage of time milder.

In addition to the Water Projects it leaves many literary works practically about to be edited, something that will be sought in the public light.

In memoriam

IDEAS FOR A PROJECT TO TAKE ADVANTAGE OF THE PANTANOSAN PLAINS OF THE HIGH ZAMBEZI

and

CULTIVATION OF THE ALUVIAL PLAIN OF LOWER ZAMBEZI

CHAPTERS:

ONE

POLITICAL TENSIONS.

At present (*1984) the Southern African States, subject to a strong economic crisis, are in need of mitigating their external tensions, since their internal tensions are very strong. Internal conflicts demand absolute attention. But there is a risk that if internal problems cannot be resolved and they exceed a certain limit, an exit is sought, a deviation from internal problems through the development of external conflicts, whether spontaneous or artificial. Here is the most common cause of wars.

Such is the risk we try to take care of. As is known, politics must anticipate conflicts, taking care of their effects and, for this, it is necessary to anticipate them. Politics cannot tow events; You need to anticipate, know your evolution.

Under the current conditions of the subcontinent, the foreseeable evolution cannot be bleaker. The peculiarities of the African society, the economic crisis, the overpopulation, the immaturity of the States and, above all, the existence of an extremely anomalous political situation in the Republic of South Africa (*1984*), are factors whose result has to be disastrously disastrous. Only the intervention of new factors, which break the vicious circle, can promote a radical turn and that the result, over time, will be different.

TWO

CLIMATE CONTRASTS.

In past centuries, for European merchants, the African continent was an inhospitable and strange land. Great climatic contrasts, always under the common denominator of overwhelming heat, long stages of excessive humidity and excessive dryness. Months raining daily, followed by long seasons without rain. In most of the territory the most radical transformations of Nature occur regularly, that changes from a large garden to a desolate wasteland.

Europeans were used to less extreme weather. His settlement on the continent collided with notable difficulties. The African case is different from that of other tropical lands - Asia, America - because here the contrast is less pronounced, it is compensated by climatic factors that do not take these long stages of devastating droughts so far; Thus, in the other continents, this phenomenon only occurs in limited territories, being in Africa the general rule.

The European adaptation had to be limited to certain highlands, of regular rains and less pronounced droughts. More than the heat itself, with its sequel to diseases, it has been the phenomenon of drought that has limited the roots of the European population in Africa. In those centuries -XV to XVIII- the continent was half empty and there was land for everyone, which would not be the case later.

THREE

INESTABILITY.

The fact that most of the continent suffers a very dry annual period has caused that the native populations, being adapted to the climatic environment, are frequently exposed to the limit of survival. Faced with the danger of consumption, they must leave some territories that allow them to survive. Constant migrations occur. Only in a few territories we find, in the past, perennially established populations. The space occupied by each town was much larger than the one that actually inhabited and within it he moved according to humidity, that is, fertility to obtain crops and raise herds. It is a different form of nomadism and transhumance. It is a nomadism is a limited space, but extensive, that each town has to reserve by necessity. Thus, there is a constant transfer of peoples, similar to what happened at the outer borders of the Roman Empire in central and eastern Europe. In such a way that the fixed settlements, the cities, and with it the development of the civilization of continuous form are missing.

While the African peoples have not established themselves in a stable manner, a cycle of civilization has not been able to begin.

FOUR

INGRAIN.

This problem is still latent today, despite the establishment of fixed borders. During the colonial era, which ended just two decades ago (* 1984), that situation remained unchanged. It is the first mission of the current states to root populations in their homelands and end with millenary instability. For this, it is necessary to overcome the difficulties that Nature imposes and have been the cause of this millenary uprooting, extracting from the lands all the resources they can give. The techniques of the Egyptian, Greco-Roman and Arabic civilizations have been acting on the continent, without the problem having been solved more than partially.

Only modern western hydraulic engineering can achieve definitive results on the continent. It is in this sense that we make the proposal, referring to a limited space, but capable of absorbing and sustaining large populations. This could be a first step, which would have a great effect on all the Zambezi countries. It is necessary, then, that modern hydraulic engineering be applied in an exhaustive manner, since only it can correct the disastrous moisture-dryness contrasts, which are the cause of the miseries suffered by the African continent.

FIVE

THE SWAMPS OF OKAWANGO.

These swampy plains are at a height slightly higher than the Zambezi course, in Botswana territory. They drain spontaneously towards another swampy region, located to the southeast, the salt flats of Makarikari; however, intermittently they also pour into Zambezi himself. The Okawango or Cubango is an Angolan river that should flow into the Zambezi, but it finds a vast flat plain through which it spreads its waters, forming a permanent, shallow swamp, which is neither a lake nor manages to open a channel to the great river, since its flow is insufficient for it, due to the great extension of this plain. On the other hand, this plain, instead of leaning to the Zambezi River, has an even lower point to the southeast, where the waters escape from which they should form a river course to the Zambezi, in the northeast direction. With the normal floods the waters pour into Makarikari and with the exceptional ones they reach the main river. The swamps are neither lake nor agricultural space.

They currently serve very little; Only some fishing villages live in it. Modifying the situation is what we propose in the present study. To turn it into an agricultural space, it is enough to end this ambiguous situation, since it is neither lake nor ceases to be. It's about stopping it altogether. To do this, the flood water must be given a sufficient exit, opening a channel that drains into the Zambezi, also facilitating the exit to it of the Kuando river. In this way, this pale region would cease to be a barren swamp to become a large agricultural area of presumably fertile soils.

SIX

A GREAT OASIS.

For a long geological period, the waters of the Cubango have been evaporating in this region and depositing their silts there. Thus a large alluvial space of at least 30,000 square kilometres has been formed, almost as large as the Egyptian. If, by means of hydraulic works, the region was not flooded, we would have a first consequence. Rains are not enough here for a good harvest. We are in the limits of the Kalahari, that is to say, in a Sahelian territory, not only the lack of heavy rains, but subject to marked contrasts of dryness. This is the characteristic of the Sahelian climate: the great irregularity of the rains. Irrigation is imposed, because it is necessary to compensate for the droughts. In this way, in addition to facilitating the exit of the general flood, it would be necessary to channel part of these flood waters during the rainy season to the floodplains, irrigating them. Thus, a good harvest would be obtained during the rainy season.

SEVEN

THE COUNTRY OF THE BAROTSE.

Through the drainage of the plain and the contribution of a part of the flow of the rivers that flood it, an annual harvest could be obtained. But it would be possible to get a second harvest, during the dry season, from the swamps of Upper Zambezi, if the waters of the great river were retained and diverted to the swamps of Okawango.

Through a canal, a part of the waters of the headwaters of the Zambezi could be brought here from the streams of Ngonya or from above. Thus, we could achieve continued cultivation of this region.

EIGHT

THE ZAMBEZI.

The Zambezi is a special case in geography. It runs first through a flat plateau where he and his tributaries lose most of their flow. It is a fairly rainy region, with 1,500 mm, in the northern part and 1,000 mm, in the central. The volumetric flow in the Victoria waterfall is 1,100 cubic meters per second. But the rains that fall in the region would allow to expect an average contribution of 3,000 to 4,000 cubic meters per second. In the same way as the Nile in the Sudan, the Zambezi in its upper part loses the ¾ parts of its water. A complementary task, then, could be done in this regard, recovering water that would be a benefit, if it did not evaporate.

First, water for agriculture in the plains of the Okawango; second, water to produce energy in the electric stations located below.

Rivers like the Zambezi, the Yellow, the Nile, when they pass through arid regions or with a long dry season, lose much of their waters. Thus, Yellow River has 3,000 cubic meters in Lanchou, at the exit of Tibet, and 1,500 when it enters the Great Plain. On this particularity of the Nile we have done a monographic study and a proposal based on the recovery of its waters.

NINE

SALOBRES LAGOONS: MAKARIKARI AND ETOSHA.

The salt marshes of Makarikari, where the leftovers of the waters that flood the Okawango region through the Botletle River are going to be lost, have about 10,000 square kilometres. In Namibia territory, about 500 kilometres to the west are the brackish marshes of Ethosa, fed by small rivers in the region and having about 5,000 square kilometres. In total, 15,000 square kilometres, 1.5 million hectares of alluvial land, although saline. In order to recover these lands, it would be necessary to create a system of exit of its waters and that the successive annual floods were washing the salt, until leaving the territory for the culture free.

The Etosha lagoon collects the waters of the Ovanbo Steppe and rivers from Angola and is separated from the sea by a slight ridge, of low altitude. The rivers of the desert coast have not had power so far to capture the river system located above.

The work of man should be to accelerate a process that will geologically end up occurring, giving fluvial output to this region. With this, the lagoons would not be a dead end in which salts are deposited and sterilized agricultural land. The same could be applied to the Makarikari swamps, approximately with a double extension, which are collected by the leftovers from the Okawango swamps. The point occupied by the swamps is the lowest on the plateau and giving it out is difficult. If it was possible to pour its waters, either towards the Zambezi or towards the Orange, the work we propose for the Etosha swamps could be repeated.

If it were possible to put into cultivation the territory that today occupies the lagoon of Etosha, Namibia would have an agricultural base on which to maintain itself as a State, since they are 500,000 hectares and the country has a million inhabitants *(*1984)*, largely occupied in mining holdings One of the underlying problems that cause the current instability would be resolved: the lack of food resources.

As for the brackish marshes of Makarikari, if it were possible to wash them by means of a drainage device - which could well be the conduction of its waters to the south. One million hectares of alluvial land would be earned, which would complete and expand the Okawango swamp system.

TEN

BOTSWANA.

One of the reasons why the exploitation of this territory has not been carried out until now has been that it is located in the outer limits of Botswana; but, in turn, being the point of convergence of the borders between Angola, Namibia, Zambia, Zimbabwe and Botswana itself, it is in the place furthest from the vital centres of each of those States. Botswana has 600,000 square kilometres and its population of one million inhabitants (* 1984) is concentrated in the opposite part of the territory, next to the Transvaal border.

ELEVEN

FOOD CAPACITY.

The key to the draft is in the food capacity of those alluvial lands. Its extension is, together, almost 50,000 square kilometres, 5 million hectares, more than the Egyptian oasis. One hectare of intensively cultivated land can feed a family, but a larger plot of land is needed to provide an acceptable standard of living. In any case, it is possible to install at least one million farmers in this region and, at most, three million. That is, between 5 and 10 million people could live directly from the cultivation of the land.

After agriculture or primary sector would come the remaining economic activities - industry, services -, which could greatly double this initial population. The maximum absorption capacity of this territory can be taken as 30 million people, thanks to the intensive and continuous cultivation of the land. In the Egyptian oasis, to a lesser extent, 45 million currently live (*1984*).

TWELVE

IMMIGRATORY CORE.

The total population of the subcontinent countries as a whole is 75 million people (* 1984). If 30 million could be housed in the territory we propose to colonize, this would mean that 2/5 of the population of each of them could stay here. For example, 2.5 of the 7 million Zambians; 3 of the 8 million Angolans; almost 4 of the 9 million Zimbabweans.

Finally, of the 32 million inhabitants of the Republic of South Africa, at least 12 million; But, since the Bantu population is 22 million, the result would be that in South Africa the Bantu population would be about 10 million people. This without taking into account that, if it were possible to transfer water from the Zambezi to the Orange and the Cape, along that line large irrigated oases could be created, as we will see below.

THIRTEEN

WATER FOR CAPE.

An interesting aspect of the device is the possibility of taking guide of the Zambezi to the southern regions of the subcontinent, even to the Cape Town itself, through the eastern fringe of the Kalahari. The Republic of South Africa, so well-endowed in other economic aspects, suffers from a marked lack of water. The population is concentrated in plateaus, where it rains moderately, and on the Indian coast. But at least half of the territory can be described as arid. It is precisely this arid region, at the height of the plateaus where the Zambezi and its tributaries run, that could benefit from a canal or aqueduct that will carry there the surpluses of water from those rivers, instead of letting them be miserably lost in the salt marshes of Makarikari. Thus, along a route of almost 1,000 kilometres, optimal angels could sprout in the desert. After crossing the threshold that separates the dry slopes of Makarikari and the Molopo, tributary of the Orange and nowhere exceeds 1,000 meters of altitude, water conduction is easier. The question is: Does Alto Zambezi have enough water for all that? The river and its tributaries drain the rains of a northern mountainous front of 1,200 kilometres in length, very wet. Its actual runoff is 3,000 to 4,000 cubic meters per second. It is about carrying out the drainage works so that all of that water comes out, instead of evaporating. Then this additional project would be possible, which would create a strong interdependence between the Republic of South Africa and the rest of Southern Africa.

FOURTEEN

THE UGANDESE CASE AND THE EGYPTIAN EXAMPLE.

On the northern shores of Lake Victoria was the kingdom of Buganda, which aroused great admiration among European travellers when they discovered it in the middle of the last century (* XIX), the abundance and regularity of the rains provided penguin crops. The English thought they saw here a model to apply in the rest of the African territories. At the beginning of this century (* XX), however, the British protectors had the weakness of establishing a landowner property system, while the mass of the population was subjected to a state of servitude. That situation seems to have been gradually changing and now small property predominates. However, either because of the civil war, the drought, or because of the failure of the agricultural exploitation system itself, the result has been that today their misery and chaos reign. The Okawango device and its annexes are similar, in a way, and their result could be the same. How to avoid it?

First, the system is not identical. Here it is an intensive cultivation system, with a harvest during the rainy season, by irrigation with the flooding of the rivers and the rains themselves, and a second crop with the retention at the head of the station's water rivers rainy for use in the dry. Crops could be obtained continuously. The result would be much more satisfactory; crops, safer and more abundant than in Uganda; yields, much higher per hectare. The case of Uganda should make us reflect, because African agriculture cannot be left happily exposed to the rains, to its cycles of abundance and scarcity. This must be corrected with the artificial work of man.

FIFTEEN

CORRECTING NATURE.

Natural phenomena occur according to a complicated mechanism, the result of the combination of very heterogeneous factors. This produces a mosaic of physical situations between those that man finds himself and against which he has to fight to survive. The regions in which the combination gives an optimal result for man are scarce, almost non-existent. There was the Earthly Paradise. Most often, these geographical situations contain favourable and unfavourable factors, advantages and disadvantages. While man, throughout early history, did not endow himself with means by which to counteract negative factors, he was abandoned to his fate. But culture consists precisely in that, in creating artificial means with which to correct the whims of Nature.

The contrasts between some regions and others in terms of humidity, fertility, accessibility, must be corrected, complemented. Because in Nature almost everything happens in an excessive, overabundant way. Thus, in some regions there is excessive humidity and in others, excess aridity: or a seemingly humid region actually suffers a painful oscillation of rainy and dry seasons. This is the case of the territory that concerns us. It is necessary to achieve a balance, a continuity. That is, that favourable factors, such as humidity, which occurs there in a part of the year, are distributed throughout it, so that a factor as destructive as aridity disappears.

On the other hand, in Africa fertile lands are extremely scarce due to laterization, which converts agricultural land, to considerable depth, into a cobblestone. Only in certain territories do we find land that can be easily cultivated, but most are outside the intertropical space. Among these lands, the alluvially are the most interesting. In

Southern Africa, apart from the coastal plains that have formed the rivers with their alluviums, and which are usually covered with forests, the only extensive alluvial region is that of the Okawango swamps. This presumably fertile territory, fed by tributaries of the Zambezi, is the one that would interest us to colonize. It is barely two hundredth of the total extension of the subcontinent, but due to the intensive use that could be the object, it could be of exceptional utility.

We must make the most of the few lands that in Southern Africa have natural conditions for this. Furthermore, unsuspected consequences can result from its intensive use.

The purpose of correcting Nature, artificially facilitating the factors that it does not create and counteracting the negatives, can be applied here optimally. Perennial flooding can be avoided and the land it covers and becomes unusable, put into cultivation.

SIXTEEN

DEMOGRAPHY AND MODERNITY.

Two opposing factors act on the countries of the World: on the one hand, the process of modernization and, on the other, population growth. Both factors have extreme power and fight hard. In industrialized countries, with a high standard of living, the process of modernization is going faster than population growth, although in recent years this advantage has diminished considerably, almost disappearing. But in the Third World countries it is the other factor that has considerable advantage, which is enlarged as time goes by.

Therefore, in these countries, any factor that contributes to slowing the progress of population growth, through strong action in favour of modernization, is of paramount importance. These two factors are interdependent; If one advances, the other goes back. Thus, any rapid modernization progress is projected on the demographic factor, weakening its influence.

When an intensively cultivated nucleus is created in the heart of Southern Africa, which means a strong advance in the modernization factor, there is a setback, a weakening of the tare that is for society the excessive population growth. If the thrust of this modernizing factor, with large hydraulic works, installation of population masses at a much more advanced standard of living than the current one, is very strong, the demographic pressure could be reduced until it becomes bearable. It would reach a turning point in the demographic curve, because at a higher standard of living, lower population growth. The colonization of this small territory, just 1/200 of the total extension of the subcontinent, could be the crucial point in which the result of the struggle of these two opposite factors will change sign. Up to now, modernization in these countries is clearly lagging behind and is barely able to cope with minimal progress.

The distance between the needs that demographic growth poses and those that modernizing progress is able to meet is growing. Demographic growth and, with it, the survival needs are greater than the ability to meet them that seeks the process of modernization that takes place throughout the World. But the demographic factor continues to push relentlessly, creating needs that progress cannot placate.

SEVENTEEN

DEMOCRACY AND RACISM.

We will not be able to say that the British are not democrats, nor that among them the negrofilia, the defense of the blacks has not had its main drivers. Recall, if not, the British navy's fight against slave traders in the early nineteenth century and that they were the first to abolish slavery in their colonies. Such an attitude was induced by interested causes - the substitution of labour by machines - but also by serious moral and religious imperatives. However, between desire and need there is a great abyss frequently.

The phenomenon of racism has been presented with great force in the African continent. During the colonial era the African peoples were equipped with iron weapons, and even fire, to defend themselves against European invaders. On the other hand, indigenous states were generally small and weak. The result was that, although those states easily dissolved within the colonial administration, the indigenous peoples remained forming a dense, resistant mass, refractory to the invaders. In addition, the number of targets installed on the continent was always small; the relations between the two races They were never easy. In the best case, a collaboration was reached to develop economic activities. But miscegenation, the mixture of races, was only a secondary phenomenon.

In part to justify the colonial situation, pseudo-scientific theories appeared in Europe that tried to demonstrate the superiority of the Nordeuropean race over the others. These were the times when culture in Europe and North America had an indisputable superiority. The historical fact that Western civilization, in its boom period, was located in these northern territories, led to the identification of this historical and, therefore, transitory factor, with a racial, congenital superiority: that is, eternal, definitive. According to those theories, the Nordeuropean peoples had been and would always be more creative and enterprising; the cultural creations of Semites, Hindus, Chinese, Native Americans, Mediterranean, were only an intermediate step.

This theory tried to attribute to the white towns, in their relations with the others, a superior right, an indisputable leadership. White settlers in Africa were deeply imbued with these beliefs, also fueled by capricious interpretations of religious texts. Their relations with the natives, for these reasons, were never easy, on an equal footing. There were also strong economic reasons for not being, but that mentality created a true abyss.

However, racism has very little to do with all this. Here we are faced with a social and economic situation, with a political structure. There is a white minority "surrounded" by a black majority and there is a struggle between the two ethnic groups because the minority fears being absorbed by the majority and dispossessed of their privileges.

Here the problem takes on a racial aspect and in European countries it was exclusively social, of class struggle. In South Africa, a typical oligarchic regime appears, with a minority possessing land and weapons and a marginalized majority reduced to servile status. The end of ancient Sparta is not reached, in which the Spartans themselves were barely thirty-thirds of the lacedemons. The white minority is afraid (* 1984), simply, that, in a democratic, egalitarian regime, it would lose political power and, with it, economic power. This is their distrust, which keeps the minority and majority in an unbearable situation.

Whites fear the establishment of a democratic regime for the whole

population, as long as they practice
this democracy among themselves.
But the black majority imperatively
needs the democratic system to be
established there.

EIGHTEEN

TWO POLICIES.

There is a relationship policy between the states whereby the strength of some is based on the weakness of others. A State goes against strengthening those that directly affect it and tries to weaken them. But there is another policy, more intelligent, that seeks to eliminate the reasons why a confrontation could arise. There is no interest in assaulting each other, because each one is satisfied with himself.

In this way, it is not convenient for the Republic of South Africa to have neighbors full of problems, overflowing with difficulties, which can lead to the outbreak of internal armed conflicts and, as an inevitable consequence, the establishment of military regimes. This could have unpredictable consequences for the subcontinent. The Republic of South Africa is not interested in creating a climate of belligerence in this part of the World that, although initially it would seem to guarantee its safety, would soon reach him. In this sense, the fate of the Pretoria government (*1984) is linked to that of the remaining southern states.

If the serious problems of overpopulation, lack of food resources, impotence to quickly modernize the countries and win the race to the shortage are not resolved with determination, it is impossible to expect another result. If the conflicts are generalized in the Zambezi region - and there are already some of them - they will soon manifest themselves south of the Limpopo.

NINETEEN

TURBULENCES.

We must not forget that one of the features of African society, characteristic of its idiosyncrasy, is the outbursts of turbulent, uncontrollable movements, which unexpectedly occur as a storm, which then passes, but while it remains there is no force capable of counteracting them. This was already pointed out by Hegel at the beginning of the last century (* XIX) in his Philosophy of History. The possibility of movements of this nature exploding, in case the problems are not satisfactorily resolved, is not remote. Perhaps that turbulence is the contrast, the complement, of the patient and strong temperament of the African peoples. But it is a factor that is there and we cannot ignore it.

TWENTY

JUXTAPOSED SOCIETIES.

Different societies coexist in the territory of the Republic of South Africa. They are really different states. There is a State of European origin and a State for each of the other groups: that of the Bantu majority and those of the Mestizo and Hindu-ethnic minorities. Apparently, all of them are governed by the same laws, those of the Republic. But each group has a different social, political, economic and individual situation, so that, in practice, the laws by which each group is governed are different. Each ethnic group has a specific state form. On the same territory we find this strange phenomenon established, which, on the other hand, is not new to the African continent. Travelers traveling through Nigeria at the end of the last century (* XIX) - Ortega and Gasset reminds us - observed with surprise that different ethnic groups, juxtaposed societies cohabited in the same village, each of which was governed by its own system of norms . This is the situation at the southern end of the continent.

TWENTY-ONE

MAJORITY AND MINORITY.

The social organization based on a balance between majorities and minorities has been frequent throughout history. Of course, the democratic system is that the whole society forms a single social group, in which there are no majorities or minorities. In South Africa we find a reminiscence of a past that, however, is not so far away. But here we find an abnormal situation, of which we can find few precedents. As a general rule, a balance, a concord, has been achieved between a majority and a minority or between a dominant minority and minorities or subordinate majorities. This concord was born from the economic specialization of each social group; thus, the dominant minority exclusively developed administrative, political and military activities, that is, exercised power, while the subordinate majority had a monopoly on economic activities - agriculture, manufacturing, mining, commerce - various. From this agreement, a stable coexistence was possible.

However, in the Republic of South Africa the same economic activities are carried out simultaneously by the dominant minority and by the submitted majority. Whites are farmers, miners, industrial workers, exactly the same as Bantu, except that they are governed by different labor and economic laws. That is why we indicated in the previous point that there are several juxtaposed states there. In this way there can never be a balance - that without taking into account that in a democratic system, the only one that can be considered desirable at the present time, this would be inadmissible. But, even so, there is no possibility that spontaneous concord will be achieved among the different social groups.

There is, therefore, a situation of perennial abnormality. The dominant minority exercises power, but also monopolizes lucrative economic activities. He needs the African workforce to develop them and is not able to do it himself. If whites were to carry out these economic activities exclusively, also leaving those that they cannot perform exclusively, a relatively stable situation would be achieved ... if we were in other centuries.

The origin of the colony was already marked by this star. The Boers, a word that means "peasants," were cattle farmers and needed pastures for their growing flocks; but we found the Bantu in front of us, also farmers who needed the same pastures. Later, when the gold mines were discovered, the heavy work in very bad conditions was done by those who were capable: the vigorous Bantu peoples.

TWENTY-TWO

SLAVES, SERVANTS, CITIZENS.

Not so long ago that slavery was generally admitted almost everywhere. Until the substitution of human labor for heavy work by machines, moral admonitions were of no use. Our great grandparents still lived in a world in which slavery was a common occurrence. So moralizing on this issue would be nothing more than giving evidence of Pharisaism. The slave has no individual or social rights; Their rights are mere concessions, something that does not belong to them. Slavery has taken many forms and nuances, but basically it consists in the deprivation of individual and social rights. During the contemporary era the African peoples, victims of the slave trade must collectively have as bad conscience as the whites who performed it, since these slaves were captured and sold by the African peoples among those of their race. From the shores of the two oceans this phenomenon acted towards the interior of the continent.

Thus a tremendous forced migration movement developed, which kept the continent in constant effervescence.

An intermediate form between slavery and individual freedom is servitude. The servant has some individual rights, but he lacks political rights. He can dispose of himself in his individual life and he has a financial means, but he cannot come and go as he pleases, nor can he make his opinions heard, nor intervene in public affairs, since he has no political rights, is this not Situation of the Bantu majority in the Republic of South Africa? (*1984). Lacking political rights, they have a limited capacity for movement, opinion, and cannot intervene in public affairs so that action can be effective. Are these not the traits of servitude? It seems, at first glance, that this is what hides apartheid, a camouflaged servitude situation.

Within the juxtaposition of States that occurs in that territory, there is a State in which citizens enjoy full individual rights, and there are three different racial groups with limited political rights, in a situation that cannot be qualified other than servitude, Hence the seriousness of the problem, because at this time, at the end of the twentieth century (* Written by the author in 1984), due to an accumulation of circumstances, we stumbled into this part of the World with something that seemed to belong to the past. However, the pressure that the democratic conscience exerts on the consciences of that dominant society, in which the members are citizens with full rights, means that formulas to change the situation are being sought and proof of this are the recent elections in the that, apparently, a democratic channel has been given to two minorities, but without keeping the most elementary political right: equality in electoral representation. Again, limited rights, limited freedoms.

TWENTY-THREE

DEMOGRAPHIC PRESSURE.

In the last thirty years the population of the subcontinent has more than doubled giving one of the fastest growth rates on the planet. Until now, much of the population growth has been absorbed by the creation of new industrial and commercial activities. It has long been possible to relieve the demographic weight in this way. But now we are in full industrial crisis; production has stagnated for some years and it is the developing countries that are taking the worst part in the distribution of the sacrifices. Developing countries have to wait for the industrialized to get a new push forward, which is still problematic. Developing countries, which benefited from global economic growth, now have to wait patiently for industrialized countries to solve their problems and create conditions in the Third World so that they can continue the industrialization process there as well. Meanwhile, the population has grown remarkably, and continues to do so despite the economic crisis. In these countries, it was previously a priority to establish the bases of an industrialization, the only formula to get out of underdevelopment, but at present they are, in a hurry, with a more serious problem: the lack of food resources for a population that has doubled , almost tripled. This problem right now is the essential one.

CONCLUSION

The marshes of Okawango are easily avenables, since it is at a higher altitude than the Zambezi River, towards which they pour in the very rainy years. Its alluvial soil must be fertile. It could be colonized with relative ease.

The Zambezi River and its tributaries should carry much more water than the water in Victoria waterfalls (1,100 m3 / s) and this is lost due to evaporation in the swampy plains of its upper course. It would be enough to eliminate obstacles, in the form of floods, that interrupt its channel.

The brackish marshes of Makarikari and Etosha could also be used, giving way to the waters, which would eventually drag the salts.

Between the alluvial territories of Okawango, Makarikari, Etosha, Barotse Country and oasis along the route to the Cape, the colonizable territory must have about 50,000 square kilometres, 5 million hectares.

By channeling the flood waters, a harvest can be obtained in the rainy season. Withholding water at the head of the rivers, two or more crops.

A territory of 5 million hectares, intensely cultivated, can house a considerable mass of population and produce large crops.

Surplus water, once evaporation is prevented, could be directed south and could also improve the performance of hydroelectric stations.

Installed in this region. Now almost uninhabited, large masses of inhabitants from surrounding countries, these would have an agricultural base on which to stand.

Downloaded from a part of its population, internal tensions would be reduced and states would have greater stability than at present.

The water taken to the south would create an interdependence between the Republic of South Africa and its hostile neighbors. Thus the natural conditions of agreement between the states of the subcontinent could arise.

Finally, perhaps within the Republic of South Africa, easing the pressure of the majority on the minority, it was possible to improve political relations and, finally, not feeling in danger, the Pretoria regime agreed to establish an authentic democratic system .

The story of the milkmaid? Nothing of that. There are arable land, mass food production, stress relief. Everything else depends on the initiative, on the political will.

Author's page on Amazon:

Amazon.com/author/juansanzsanz